a nervous No

a joyful No

an angry No

a timid No

a forced No

an inattentive No

Sky Pony Press books may be purchased in bulk at special discounts for sales promotion, corporate gifts, fund-raising, or educational purposes. Special editions can also be created to specifications. For details, contact the Special Sales Department, Sky Pony Press, 307 West 36th Street, 11th Floor, New York, NY 10018 or info@skyhorsepublishing.com.

Sky Pony® is a registered trademark of Skyhorse Publishing, Inc.®, a Delaware corporation.

Visit our website at www.skyponypress.com.

10 9 8 7 6 5 4 3 2 1

Manufactured in China, November 2023
This product conforms to CPSIA 2008

Library of Congress Cataloging-in-Publication Data is available on file.

Cover design by Elke Kohlmann & Kai Texel
Cover illustrations by Dagmar Geisler
US Edition edited by Nicole Frail

Print ISBN: 978-1-5107-7703-3
Ebook ISBN: 978-1-5107-7704-0

Sometimes You Have to Say No

How to Set and Respect Limitations

Written and Illustrated by
Dagmar Geisler

Translated by
Andy Jones Berasaluce

Sky Pony Press
New York

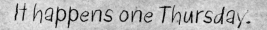

It happens one Thursday.

Ms. Rose is standing on her balcony with a cherry-covered dessert.

"Would you like a piece?" she asks. Ms. Rose is the best baker in town.

"No, thank you!" Lukas and Taya say and sigh loudly. They promised not to eat anything sweet before dinner.

"No, thanks," says Emil. He doesn't like cherries.

"No, thank you," says Matilda. She's still full from lunch.

Ms. Rose really is a cheerful lady. But now she's had enough. Why are they all saying no?

Mr. Florian from the bank had also said no to her dessert again, and this time she went to a lot of trouble to make it extra perfect. Mr. Florian declined very politely, but a no is still a no and that hurts, thinks Ms. Rose.

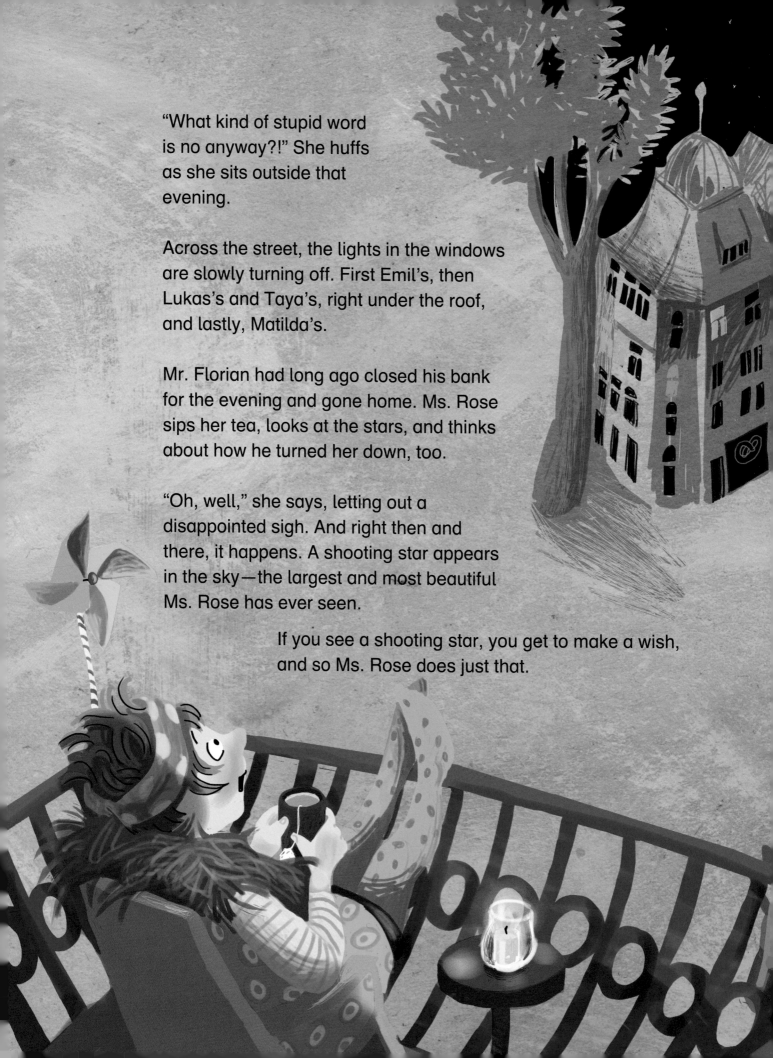

"What kind of stupid word is no anyway?!" She huffs as she sits outside that evening.

Across the street, the lights in the windows are slowly turning off. First Emil's, then Lukas's and Taya's, right under the roof, and lastly, Matilda's.

Mr. Florian had long ago closed his bank for the evening and gone home. Ms. Rose sips her tea, looks at the stars, and thinks about how he turned her down, too.

"Oh, well," she says, letting out a disappointed sigh. And right then and there, it happens. A shooting star appears in the sky—the largest and most beautiful Ms. Rose has ever seen.

If you see a shooting star, you get to make a wish, and so Ms. Rose does just that.

She wishes as hard as she can. The word "no" must disappear from the world.

"Nobody needs it!" she says, blows out her candle, and goes to bed.

The next morning, the sun is shining in the sky, the birds are chirping, and a light wind blows the scent of flowers into the houses.

"Did you sleep well, pumpkin?" Emil's father asks. Emil didn't sleep well. There was a mosquito in his room, it buzzed nonstop, and, on top of that, it'd bit him.

"No," he wants to say, but the word won't come out. "So-so," he says instead and then burns his tongue on his hot chocolate. *Ugh!*

Next door, Lukas and Taya are also having breakfast, and, like almost every morning, Taya annoys her brother a little.

"Would you like sausage in your cereal?" teases Taya.

Taya expects
Lukas to grow
irritated and yell,
"No way!"

Then Taya would say
something like, "Why not? It tastes
so good!" She'd giggle and wave the
sausage over his cereal again.

That's how the game is supposed to go.

But today, Lukas says nothing. Nothing at all.

Taya looks at him, confused, and then she lets the sausage plop into
the cereal and strawberries. What else is she supposed to do?

Nobody can say the word "no." Shaking their heads no longer works, and when Ms. Heilmann from the bookstore tries to experiment with a few written sentences one can use to reject something in a different way, that doesn't work either. It's impossible to write the word, and there's no way to express it that works.

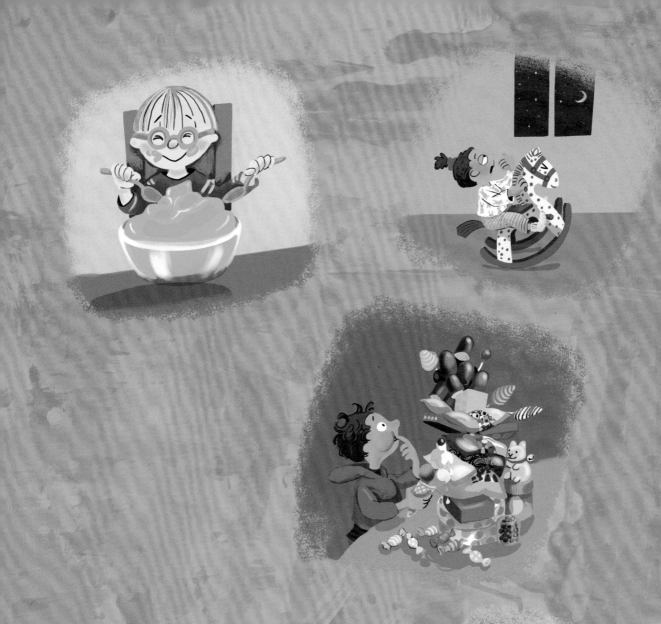

The children find it quite funny and ask all the questions that their parents would almost always say no to.

"May I have big bowl of green Jell-O for dinner?" Emil asks his father.

Taya asks Mama and Papa if she can stay up as late as she wants.

Lukas always wants sweets, and Matilda asks for so many bedtime stories that her mother becomes very hoarse.

The children are amazed at how quickly they get bored, and then they realize that there are many situations in which you desperately need to be able to say no.

"This can't go on," says Emil.

"Yes!" shouts Lukas. "Something has to happen. Taya won't dare go outside since that weird guy tried to chat her up."

"We're getting our Nnnnn . . . back!" Taya yells. Her face turns quite red from exertion. But she can't get out more than the N.

"But how's that going to happen?" asks Matilda. "We don't even know where it went."

"Then we just have to find out!" says Taya.

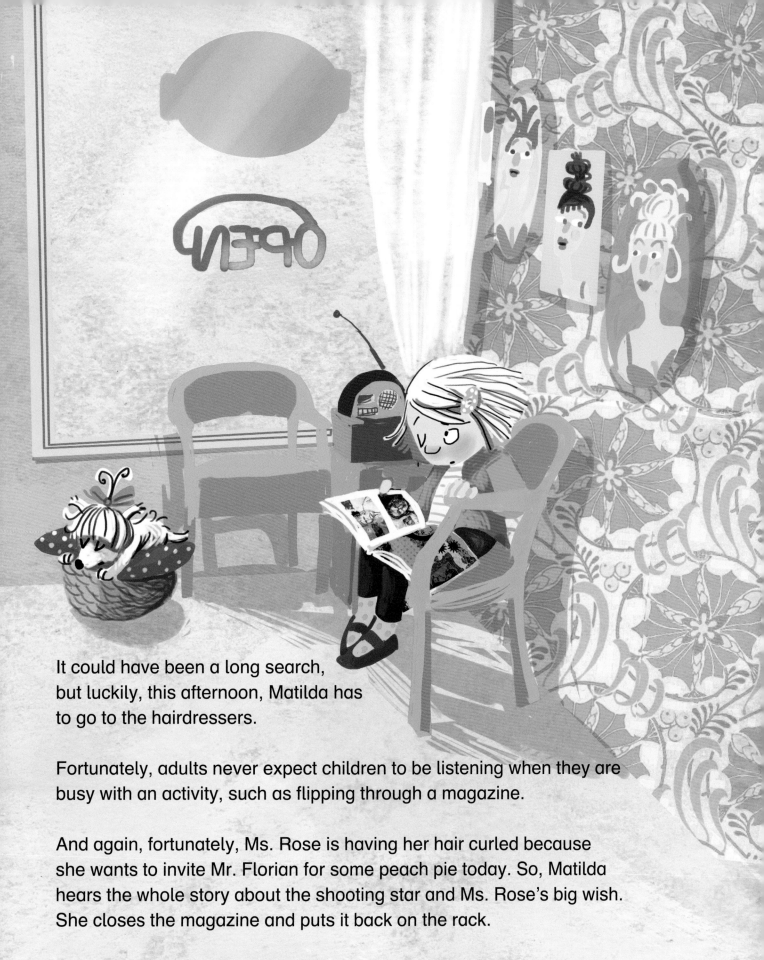

It could have been a long search,
but luckily, this afternoon, Matilda has
to go to the hairdressers.

Fortunately, adults never expect children to be listening when they are
busy with an activity, such as flipping through a magazine.

And again, fortunately, Ms. Rose is having her hair curled because
she wants to invite Mr. Florian for some peach pie today. So, Matilda
hears the whole story about the shooting star and Ms. Rose's big wish.
She closes the magazine and puts it back on the rack.

There's no time for haircuts now.

When Matilda goes to the others with her news, they also have news for Matilda.

"We figured out how to get the Nnn . . . past our lips!" exclaims Emil.

"You just have to sing it," says Taya.

"Off to Ms. Rose's then!" shouts Matilda.

The four of them cause a real ruckus. Lukas bangs pot lids while Emil drums with full fanfare.

Ms. Rose comes out onto the balcony and the four of them sing as loud as they can.

It might sound a little off-key, but that doesn't matter.

Ms. Rose must understand what's at stake.

We want No back,
Or it's joy we will lack.
No can have a good effect,
Used right, it can protect.
We ask, with all this fuss,
For you to give it back to us!

We want No back,
Or it's joy we will lack.
No can make us stronger,
It can't be missing for much longer.
We need it so badly, thus,
You must give it back to us!

Ms. Rose hears their song, and she invites them in to explain why they feel it's so important to sometimes say no. She understands that you can't say yes to desserts if you've promised not to eat anything sweet before dinner. And she understands why being able to say no can be vital. She puts her hands in front of her face. She can't even imagine the dangers she has put the children in. And she, herself, would've actually liked to say no when the hairdresser asked if she wanted a few green and purple highlights in her hair.

"By the way," says Emil, "Mr. Florian is allergic to sweets."

Matilda nods. "He'll never say yes to dessert."

"Dear me!" says Ms. Rose, and she lets out a sad sob. "What are we going to do now?" she asks, looking helplessly at the others.

Lukas has an idea. That evening they all meet at Ms. Rose's and keep an eye out for shooting stars. They wait and wait.

"It won't work," says Matilda.

"There!" Emil calls out suddenly.

And, sure enough, there are shooting stars in the sky. A rainstorm of shooting stars is falling. Ms. Rose gasps. She wishes even harder than the first time.

And everyone (even Taya, who is almost asleep) wishes alongside her, strengthening the wish.

The next morning, Papa asks Emil: "Did you sleep well?"

"No!" exclaims Emil happily. That said, he slept like a log.

And Taya asks Lukas: "Would you like a booger in your cereal?"

"No, definitely not!" Lukas bellows and then he hugs his little sister so tightly that she gasps for air.

Matilda asks her mother a ton of questions: "Can you tie a knot with your nose?" and "Have you ever walked upside down on the ceiling?" And with every no, she dances with joy around the room.

Meanwhile, Ms. Rose pages through a cookbook. "Cheese casserole . . . or onion-and-bacon tart. He'll definitely like that." Then she closes the book. "I think I have to go shopping."

Ms. Rose is very excited as she walks across the square.

She waves to the children, and the children wave back.
But someone else is waving, too.

It's Mr. Florian.

"How great to run into you," he says. "Unfortunately, I'm
not into sweets, but I make the best onion tart in town.
May I invite you to have some?"

Astonished, Ms. Rose doesn't know how to respond.

"You have to say something now!" Taya calls out.

And then Ms. Rose smiles. "Well, I wouldn't say no," she
says, winking at the children.

"Does that mean yes?" asks Emil.

"That's exactly what it means," Ms. Rose replies, and
everyone feels it, all the way down to their toes:

A yes only feels good when you can also say no.

a friendly
No

a defiant
No

a self-confident No

a
defensive
No

a moody
No

a
frightened
No

an embarrassed No